Filastrocche Italiane Vol. 2

Italian Nursery Rhymes Vol. 2

Illustrated by Julie Weaver

Filastrocche Italiane Volume 2 – Italian Nursery Rhymes Volume 2

Illustrations by Julie Weaver
Translation and Design by Claudia Cerulli
Copyright © 2010 Long Bridge Publishing. All rights reserved.

All rights reserved. No part of this publication may be reproduced or transmitted in any form or by any means, electronic or mechanical, including photocopy, recording, or any information storage and retrieval system, without permission in writing from the publisher.

Visit "I Read Italian" for more books and resources for bilingual children:
www.longbridgepublishing.com

Trova tanti altri testi di narrativa bilingue nel sito: www.longbridgepublishing.com

Publisher's Cataloging in Publication data

Filastrocche Italiane Volume 2 – Italian Nursery Rhymes Volume 2
illustrated by Julie Weaver
    p.   cm.
Includes index.
SUMMARY: Fully illustrated collection of over twenty traditional Italian nursery rhymes, children's songs and tongue twisters, each one followed by the English translation, notes and instructions on how to play.
ISBN-13: 978-0-9842723-3-4
ISBN-10: 0-9842723-3-x
1. Nursery rhymes--Juvenile fiction 2. Nursery rhymes, Italian 3. Italian language materials --Bilingual.
I. Title

Long Bridge Publishing
USA
www.LongBridgePublishing.com

ISBN-13: 978-0-9842723-3-4
ISBN-10: 0-9842723-3-x

Indice – Contents

Filastrocche e ninne nanne – *Nursery rhymes and lullabies*
- C'era una volta un Re – *Once upon a time there was a King* ✳ page 5
- Ninna nanna di Frà Simon – *Brother Simon's lullaby* ✳ page 7
- Seta moneta – *Silk money* ✳ page 9
- Alla fonte del Re – *At the King's fountain* ✳ page 11
- La pigrizia – *Laziness* ✳ page 13
- Lucciola, lucciola – *Firefly, firefly* ✳ page 15
- Trucci, trucci cavallucci – *Trucci, trucci little horses* ✳ page 17
- Filastrocca delle dita – *Finger rhyme* ✳ page 19

Filastrocche per giocare – *Play rhymes*
- Giro giro tondo – *Spin, spin around* ✳ page 21
- Colombina la messaggera – *Columbine the messenger* ✳ page 23
- Madama Doré – *Madame Doré* ✳ page 25
- Oh, che bel castello! – *What a fine castle!* ✳ page 27

Filastrocche cantate – *Children's songs*
- Nella vecchia fattoria – *On the old farm* ✳ page 29
- Frà Martino – *Brother Martin ("Frère Jacques")* ✳ page 31
- Maramao – *Maramao* ✳ page 33

Scioglilingua – *Tongue twisters*
- Sopra la panca – *On the bench* ✳ page 34
- Apelle – *Apelle* ✳ page 35
- 33 Trentini – *33 Citizens of Trento* ✳ page 35
- Il cane pazzo – *The crazy dog* ✳ page 36
- Taglia l'aglio – *Chop the garlic* ✳ page 36
- Il papa e il pepe – *Pope and pepper* ✳ page 36

One more rhyme: Filastrocca dei mesi – *Nursery rhyme of the months* ✳ page 37

One more song: Tanti auguri a te – *Best wishes to you (Happy Birthday to you)* ✳ page 39

Please note that the English text following each Italian rhyme has the sole purpose of translating the Italian verses as accurately as possible. In choosing the words for the translation, the author has elected to preserve the original meaning of the verses rather than recreate rhyming sounds in English or use the English version of the same rhyme whenever this existed.

C'era una volta un Re

C'era una volta un Re
seduto sul sofà
che disse alla sua serva:
"Raccontami una storia"
e la serva cominciò:
"C'era una volta un Re
seduto sul sofà..."

What it means:

Once upon a time there was a King
who sat on a sofa
and said to his maid:
"Tell me a story"
and she said:
"Once upon a time there was a King
who sat on a sofa..."

This rhyme can go on and on...
To make it more fun, the story-teller can change the tone of her voice
every time she starts over, or she can slowly decrease the volume to a whisper.

Ninna Nanna di Frà Simon

Din don, din don.
La campana di Frà Simon,
eran due che la sonavan,
pane e vin i' domandavan.

Din don, campanon.
La campana di Frà Simon la sonava nott'e dì:
che il giorno l'è finì ed è ora di dormir.
Din don, din don.

What it means:

Ding dong, ding dong.
Brother Simon's bell,
two men were ringing it,
asking for bread and wine.

Ding dong, big bell.
Brother Simon's bell rang night and day:
the day is over and it's time to sleep.
Ding dong, ding dong.

Lullaby

Seta moneta

Seta moneta,
le donne di Gaeta che filano la seta.
La seta e la bambagia, a voi chi vi piace?
Ci piace Giovanni che fa cantare i galli.
I galli e le galline, con tutti i pulcini.
Guarda nel pozzo, che c'è un gallo rosso.
Guarda in alto, che c'è un gallo bianco.
Guarda sul letto, che c'è un bel confetto.
Guarda lassù, che c'è un cuccurucù.

What it means:

Silk money,
the women of Gaeta who spin silk.
Silk and cotton wool, who do you like?
We like Giovanni who makes the roosters sing.
The roosters and the hens, with all the chicks.
Look in the well, there's a red rooster.
Look up, there's a white rooster.
Look on the bed, there's a fine sugared almond.
Look up there, there's a cock-a-doodle-doo.

Alla fonte del Re

Alla fonte del Re
c'eran tre oche che andavano a bè.
Tre oche, due oche,
un'oca, un ochino, un ochè.
Alla fonte del Re,
c'eran quattr'oche che andavano a bè.
Quattr'oche, tre oche, due oche,
un'oca, un ochino, un ochè.
Alla fonte del Re,
c'eran cinque oche che andavano a bè.
Cinque oche, quattr'oche, tre oche, due oche,
un'oca, un ochino, un ochè…

What it means:

At the King's fountain
3 ducks went to drink.
3 ducks, 2 ducks,
1 duck, a duckling, a little duck.
At the King's fountain
4 ducks went to drink.
4 ducks, 3 ducks, 2 ducks
1 duck, a duckling, a little duck.
At the King's fountain
5 ducks went to drink.
5 ducks, 4 ducks, 3 ducks, 2 ducks,
1 duck, a duckling, a little duck…

La pigrizia

La pigrizia andò al mercato
ed un cavolo comprò.
Mezzogiorno era suonato
quando a casa ritornò.
Mise l'acqua, accese il fuoco
si sedette, riposò.
Ed intanto, a poco a poco,
anche il sole tramontò.
Così, persa ormai la lena,
sola al buio ella restò
ed a letto senza cena
la meschina se ne andò.

What it means:

Laziness went to the market
and bought a cabbage.
It was past noon
when she returned home.
She prepared the water on the stove,
sat down and rested.
In the meantime, little by little,
the sun went down.
After losing all her energy,
she ended up in the dark all alone,
and to bed without supper
she had to go.

Lucciola lucciola

Lucciola lucciola, gialla gialla,
metti la briglia alla cavalla
che la vuole il figlio del Re.
Lucciola, lucciola vieni con me.

What it means:

*Yellow yellow, firefly firefly,
bridle the filly
'cause the King's son wants her.
Firefly, firefly come with me.*

Children chant this rhyme when they chase fireflies.
There are several variations of this rhyme all over Italy, but they all have the same objective: to lure fireflies and to catch them.

Trucci, trucci cavallucci

Trucci, trucci cavallucci,
chi è che va a cavallo?
È il re del Portogallo.
Chi lo porta?
La cavalla zoppa.
Chi l'ha zoppicata?
La stanga della porta.
Dov'è la porta?
L'ha bruciata il fuoco.
Dov'è il fuoco?
L'ha spento l'acqua.
Dov'è l'acqua?
L'ha bevuta il bue.
Dov'è il bue?
Il bue è in campagna…
e mangia noci e castagne!

What it means:

Trucci trucci little horses,
Who is riding a horse?
The king of Portugal.

(Please turn the page for the rest of the translation)

Who is carrying him?
It's a lame mare.
Who made her lame?
The door bar.
Where is the door?
The fire burned it.
Where is the fire?
The water put it out.
Where is the water?
The ox drank it.
Where is the ox?
The ox is in the country...
and eats walnuts and chestnuts!

How to play:

Have the child sit over an adult's knees as if riding a horse. Child and adult should be face to face and should be holding hands.

The adult recites the rhyme and, for every line, mimics the galloping of a horse by moving his/her knees up and down, bouncing the child.

While saying the last two lines, the adult opens his/her knees and lets the child sink down a bit, while still holding the child's hands.

Filastrocca delle dita

Dice il pollice: "Ho fame!"
Dice l'indice: "Non c'è più pane."
Dice il medio: "Che faremo?"
E l'anulare: "Lo ruberemo!"
Ma il mignolo dice: "No,
io a rubare non ci sto!"

What it means:

The thumb says, "I am hungry!"
The index finger says, "There is no more bread."
The middle finger says, "What shall we do?"
And the ring finger says, "We'll steal it!"
But the pinky says: "No,
I will not steal!"

How to play:

Use this finger rhyme to teach a child the names of each finger.

Hold the child's hand and touch each finger while you say the corresponding line.

Giro, Giro, Tondo

Giro giro tondo,
casca il mondo,
casca la terra:
tutti giù per terra!

What it means:

Spin, spin around,
the world falls down,
the earth falls down:
everybody on the ground!

This is a playground singing game that corresponds to the English "Ring around the Rosie".

Colombina la messaggera

Colombina la messaggera cerca, cerca la Primavera,
la più bella che ci sia me la voglio portare via.
Ecco qui che l'ha trovata, tutta bella incipriata,
con le scarpe di cioccolata, Colombina vuol ballar.
È la sera di Carnevale, Colombina vuol ballare
e si fece accompagnare da un vecchio Barbablù
che saresti proprio tu!

What it means:

*Columbine, the messenger is searching, searching for Spring,
the most beautiful of all, I want to take her with me.
Here she is, she found her with her face all powdered,
her chocolate shoes, Columbine wants to dance.
It is the evening of Carnival (Fat Tuesday), Columbine wants to dance
and she is chaperoned by an old Bluebeard
which is you!*

How to play:

Children sing this song during Carnival (Fat Tuesday or Mardi Gras), while they play a game like "Ring-around-the Rosie". All the children wear a costume.

One child stands in the center of the ring and has to pick another child to take his/her place before the end of the song. Then the second child replaces the first one, and the song starts all over.

Madama Doré

Oh quante belle figlie, Madama Doré,
oh quante belle figlie.
Son belle e me le tengo, Scudiero del Re,
son belle e me le tengo.
Il Re ne vorrebbe una, Madama Doré,
il Re ne vorrebbe una.
Che cosa ne vuol fare, Scudiero del Re,
che cosa ne vuol fare?
La vuole maritare, Madama Doré,
la vuole maritare.
Con chi la mariterebbe, Scudiero del Re,
con chi la mariterebbe?
Col principe di Spagna, Madama Doré,
col principe di Spagna.
E come la vestirebbe, Scudiero del Re,
e come la vestirebbe?
Di rose e di viole, Madama Doré,
di rose e di viole.
Prendete la più bella, Scudiero del Re,
prendete la più bella.

(Turn the page for translation and notes)

What it means:

*Oh how many beautiful daughters, Madame Doré,
oh how many beautiful daughters.*

    *They are beautiful and I'm keeping them to myself, King's Squire,
they are beautiful and I'm keeping them to myself.*

*The King would like one of them, Madame Doré,
the King would like one of them.*

    *What does he want to do with her, King's Squire,
what does he want to do with her?*

*He wants to give her a husband, Madame Doré,
he wants to give her a husband.*

    *Whom would he marry her to, King's Squire,
whom would he marry her to?*

*To the Prince of Spain, Madame Doré,
to the Prince of Spain.*

    *And how would he dress her, King's Squire,
how would he dress her?*

*He would dress her with roses and violets, Madame Doré,
he would dress her with roses and violets.*

    *Take the most beautiful one, King's Squire,
take the most beautiful one.*

How to play:

The children form two rows facing each other; each child in a row has his/her arms interlocked. One row is the king's party and the other one is Madame Doré's party. Each row takes turns singing a line of the rhyme. The king's party begins, followed by Madame Doré's, simulating a conversation. As they sing, the children step forward and backward. At the end of the song, the king's party chooses one child from Madame Doré's party. This is repeated until all the children from Madame Doré's row have been chosen except for one, who is Madame Doré herself.

Oh, che bel castello!

Oh che bel castello, marcondiro ndiro ndello,
oh che bel castello, marcondiro ndiro ndà!
Il nostro è ancor più bello, marcondiro ndiro ndello,
il nostro è ancor più bello, marcondiro ndiro ndà!
E noi lo ruberemo, marcondiro ndiro ndello,
e noi lo ruberemo, marcondiro ndiro ndà!
E noi lo rifaremo, marcondiro ndiro ndello,
e noi lo rifaremo, marcondiro ndiro ndà!

What it means:

What a fine castle, marcondiro ndiro ndello (nonsense words),
what a fine castle, marcondiro ndiro ndà!
Ours is even better, marcondiro ndiro ndello,
ours is even better, marcondiro ndiro ndà!
And we will steal it, marcondiro ndiro ndello,
and we will steal it, marcondiro ndiro ndà!
And we will re-build it, marcondiro ndiro ndello,
and we will re-build it, marcondiro ndiro ndà!

How to play:

Two groups of children form two circles and spin around holding hands (like in "Ring around the Rosie"). One group has only two children; the other group has the remaining children. The groups take turns singing the rhymes, like in a conversation, spinning around while they sing. At the end of the rhyme one child from the large group joins the small group. Then the children start singing the rhyme all over. The purpose of the game is to "steal" the children from the large group one by one till the group that had the most children ends up with only two. There are several variations to this game, but this is one of the most popular.

Nella vecchia fattoria

Nella vecchia fattoria, ia-ia-o,
quante bestie ha zio Tobia, ia-ia-o.
C'è il cane (bau), cane (bau), ca-ca-cane (bau).
Nella vecchia fattoria, ia-ia-o,
quante bestie ha zio Tobia, ia-ia-o.
C'è il gatto (miao), gatto (miao), ga-ga-gatto (miao).
Nella vecchia fattoria, ia-ia-o,
quante bestie ha zio Tobia, ia-ia-o.
C'è la mucca (muu), mucca (muu),
mu-mu-mucca, (muu).
Nella vecchia fattoria, ia-ia-o...

What it means:

On the old farm, ee-i-ee-i-o,
how many animals Uncle Tobias has, ee-i-ee-i-o.
There's the dog (bow), dog (bow), d-d-dog (bow).
On the old farm, ee-i-ee-i-o,
how many animals Uncle Tobias has, ee-i-ee-i-o.
There's the cat (meow), cat (meow), c-c-cat (meow).
On the old farm, ee-i-ee-i-o,
how many animals Uncle Tobias has, ee-i-ee-i-o.
There's the cow (mooo), cow (mooo), c-c-cow (mooo).
On the old farm, ee-i-ee-i-o...

This is the Italian version of the famous children's song "Old McDonald Had a Farm".

Frà Martino

Frà Martino,
campanaro,
dormi tu?
Dormi tu?
Suona le campane,
suona le campane!
Din, don, dan,
din, don, dan.

What it means:

Brother Martin,
bell ringer,
are you sleeping?
Are you sleeping?
Ring the bells,
ring the bells!
Ding, dong, dang,
ding, dong, dang.

This is the Italian version of the world famous children's song known in French as "Frère Jacques".

Maramao

Maramao, perché sei morto?
Pan e vin non ti mancava,
l'insalata era nell'orto
e una casa avevi tu!
Maramao, perché sei morto?

What it means:

Maramao, why did you die?
You had wine and bread,
you had salad in the garden,
and you had a home!
Maramao, why did you die?

This is a traditional rhyme that was turned into a popular Italian song in 1939.

Scioglilingua
Tongue twisters

Sopra la panca la capra campa,
sotto la panca la capra crepa.

What it means:
On the bench the goat lives,
under the bench the goat dies.

Apelle, figlio di Apollo,
fece una palla di pelle di pollo.
Tutti i pesci vennero a galla
per vedere quella palla di pelle di pollo
fatta da Apelle figlio di Apollo

What it means:

Apelle, son of Apollo,
made a ball of chicken skin.
All the fish rose to the surface
to see the ball of chicken skin
made by Apelle, son of Apollo.

Trentatré Trentini entrarono a Trento,
tutti e trentatré trotterellando.

What it means:

Thirty three citizens of Trento entered Trento,
all thirty three trotting.

Scioglilingua
Tongue twisters

Sotto il mio palazzo
c'è un povero cane pazzo.
Date un pezzo di pane
a quel povero pazzo cane.

*Under my building
there is a poor crazy dog.
Give a piece of bread
to that poor crazy dog.*

Sul tagliere l'aglio taglia.
Non tagliare la tovaglia!
La tovaglia non è aglio,
se la tagli, fai uno sbaglio.

*Cut the garlic on the cutting board.
Don't you cut the tablecloth!
The tablecloth is not garlic,
if you cut it, you make a mistake.*

Il Papa pesa e pesta il pepe a Pisa
e Pisa pesa e pesta il pepe al Papa.

*The Pope weighs and grinds pepper in Pisa
and Pisa weighs and grinds pepper for the Pope.*

... one more rhyme:

Filastrocca dei mesi

Gennaio freddoloso,
febbraio spiritoso,
marzo pazzerello,
aprile mite e bello,
maggio sognatore,
giugno cantatore,
luglio nuotatore,
agosto gran signore,
settembre grappolaio,
ottobre castagnaio,
novembre triste e stanco,
dicembre tutto bianco.

What it means:

*Cold January,
funny February (in Italy this is the month of Carnival),
crazy March,
mild and pretty April,
May the dreamer,
June the singer,
July the swimmer,
August the gentleman,
September brings the grapes,
October brings the chestnuts,
sad and tired November,
all white December.*

... one more song:

Tanti auguri a te

Tanti auguri a te!
Tanti auguri a te!
Tanti auguri (nome del bambino),
tanti auguri a te!

What it means:

Best wishes to you!
Best wishes to you!
Best wishes to (child's name),
best wishes to you!

This is the Italian version of the world famous song "Happy Birthday to You".

Stretta è la foglia,
larga è la via,
dite la vostra
ché ho detto la mia.

*Narrow is the leaf,
broad is the way,
tell yours
for I have told mine.*

www.ingramcontent.com/pod-product-compliance
Lightning Source LLC
Chambersburg PA
CBHW041432040426
42450CB00021B/3470